I AM
GREAT

Copyright © 2017 by Nora Shariff-Borden. All rights reserved. This book or any portion thereof may not be reproduced or used in any manner whatsoever without the express written permission of the publisher except for the use of brief quotations in a book review.

Printed in the United States of America

First Printing, 2017

ISBN 978-0-9969246-1-0

Book Design: The Savvy Peach, LLC

I dedicate this book to my grandchildren. May you always have the love of Christ in your heart! I pray that you will always realize that your are great!

To my amazing husband thank you for always believing in me and encouraging me to pursue my dreams.

A NOTE FROM THE AUTHOR

I am thankful to God for giving me visions that inspire others. I love to write, and one of the reasons I believe I am so passionate about writing is because someone once told me that I would never be successful at writing. Every time I think of that statement it empowers me to write more.

My purpose for writing this book is to share with young people, that no matter what anyone says, I want them to know that they can become whatever they want and set their minds to! I also want them to remember that there is *power* in the spoken word.

I believe if they learn these principles early in life, they will become whatever they desire to be!

I AM
GREAT

I AM BEAUTIFUL

Today I will say I am beautiful!

You are altogether beautiful, my love; there is no flaw in you!
Song of Solomon 4:7

I AM HANDSOME

Today I will say
I am handsome!

For I am made by God.
Psalms 139:14

I AM GREAT

Today I will say I am great!

For greater is He that is in me than he that is in the world.
1 John 4:4

I AM POWERFUL

Today I will say I am powerful!

I will be strong in the Lord and in His Mighty Power.
Ephesians 6:10

I AM COURAGEOUS

Today I will say I am courageous!

Be strong and courageous. Do not fear for it is the Lord your God who goes (is) with you.
Deuteronomy 31:6

I AM AUTHENTIC

Today I will say I am authentic!

You are the light of the world.
Matthew 5:14

I AM WISE

Today I will say I am wise!

The wisdom that comes from Heaven is good.
James 3:17

I AM LOVED

Today I will say
I am loved!

*How do I know what Love is. Jesus laid down His life for me.
I will not love with words or speech but with words of action
and in truth.
1 John 3:17-18*

I AM KIND

Today I will say I am kind!

I will treat others the way I want to be treated.
Luke 6:31

I AM THANKFUL

Today I will say
I am thankful!

I will give thanks to the Lord because He is good!
Psalm 107:1

I AM A WINNER

Today I will say I am a winner!

I can do all things through Christ who strengthens me!
Philippians 4:13

I AM A DREAMER

Today I will say I am a dreamer!

*I will instruct you and teach you in the way you should go
I will watch over you I will guide you with my eyes!*
Psalm 32:8

I AM A BIG THINKER

Today I will say I am a big thinker!

For as you think in your heart so are you!
Proverbs 23:7

I AM WHATEVER I SAY

Today I will say who I am!

There is life and death in the power of the tongue!
Proverbs 18:21

I AM A POWERFUL CHILD OF GOD

Today I will say I am a powerful child of God!

For in Christ we are all children of God through faith!
Galatians 3:26

I AM BRAVE

Today I will say
I am brave!

Be brave. Be strong. Don't give up. Expect God to help you.
Psalm 31:24

I AM A GOAL SETTER

Today I will say I am a goal setter!

I press on toward the goal for the prize of the high calling of God in Christ Jesus.
Philippians 3:14

I AM STRONG

Today I will say I am strong!

The Lord is my strength and my shield; my heart trusts in, relies on, and leans on Him.
Psalm 28:7

I AM BLESSED

Today I will say I am blessed!

May the Lord bless you and keep you; May He make His face shine on you and be gracious to you;
Numbers 6:24-25

I AM CONFIDENT

Today I will say I am confident!

For I am confident of this very thing, that He who began a good work in you will perfect it!
Philippians 1:6

www.ingramcontent.com/pod-product-compliance
Lightning Source LLC
Chambersburg PA
CBHW061146010526
44118CB00026B/2892